MINING MEMOR

A Portrait of the Collieries of North Staffordshire

by
Fred Leigh

Foreword by Jim Worgan, Keeper of Collections,
Chatterley Whitfield Mining Museum

S. B. Publications

This book is dedicated to the valiant and hard-working miners of North Staffordshire and to the memory of the thousands who paid the ultimate price for the coal and iron that made this a great nation.

First published in 1992 by S.B. Publications,
c/o 19 Grove Road,
Seaford, East Sussex, BN25 1TP

ISBN 1. 85770. 031. 7

Typeset, printed and bound by Manchester Free Press,
Paragon Mill, Jersey St., Manchester, M4 6FP.
Tel: 061 236 8822

CONTENTS

Front Cover : Chatterley Whitfield

Title Page : Hanley Deep Pit

FOREWORD

The portrayal of the mining industry in North Staffordshire is one which I consider has been sadly neglected in the past, and it is hoped that this volume will help to rectify the situation. I am sure that there is a wealth of unpublished photographs available, and already some of those included in this book have generated tremendous interest.

The mining industry in North Staffordshire, including the small detached Cheadle Coalfield, goes back far into the mists of time, but it was only with the growth of the pottery and iron industries and the coming of the railways that mining began to expand. Before this it was basically a domestic local industry, and even with the expansion the area tended to remain a backwater until well into the twentieth century. With the need for more coal the industry began to change as pits became larger and deeper, with all the associated problems. Boreholes revealed the existence of over twenty workable seams down to a depth of 220 feet. It is interesting that all the types of coal seam found in the British Isles, with the exception of anthracite and brown coal, are present in North Staffordshire.

The landscape soon began to change with the sinking of the new deeper pits and the area was dotted with industrial eyesores, but nothing could stop the march of King Coal. Whereas most of North Staffordshire consisted of scattered communities, new mining communities, often funded by the owners, gradually grew up around the pits on which, to a large extent, the whole economy depended.

The coalfield is very rich, heavily faulted and often gassy, so at times proving difficult to work. Many disasters have occurred (as listed), and the heartbreaking scenes of women and children huddled around the pit gates are hopefully a thing of the past. Times were hard, people were poor; they often toiled long and arduous hours, sometimes in adverse conditions, often for little reward. Indeed it was considered that if anyone could work in the North Staffordshire coalfield, then he could work in any coalfield in the world.

Welfare facilities at the pits were virtually unknown until the 1930s, and I am sure that the photograph of the miner washing at home in front of the fire will evoke many memories. The community spirit was very strong and it is worth noting that it still exists today. What shone through however, and fortunately is still prevalent today, was the unique sense of camaraderie and comradeship so widespread in the industry. Men were dependent on each other at all times due to the very nature of their job, and this often extended to the communities in which they lived.

The industry has always been subject to change, which unfortunately is continuing to the present day; and who knows what the future will hold? What will remain, however, is the spirit and determination of the miners, who have always had the will to succeed, often against insurmountable odds.

I was delighted when Fred asked me to write this foreword, because I spent 32 years in the industry, all in North Staffordshire, albeit 'uptop', and considered myself very privileged and honoured to have been part of its great tradition.

Jim Worgan
Keeper of Collections
Chatterley Whitfield Mining Museum
May 1992

PREFACE

North Staffordshire is one vast coalfield. It is said that coal exists in every part of the area with the exception of the north east, where the old Namurian millstone grit of the Pennines marks the boundary of the coal measures. History reveals that there was coal-getting at Holditch in the second century. The economic way of life was changed during the life of George III, when the use of coal instead of charcoal, the rapid growth of the pottery industry, and the new arteries of transport, the canals and the railways, brought new demands for coal and iron. Pioneers of industry like Wedgwood, Granville and Heath, to name just a few, changed not only the landscape but the people themselves.

It is sad in a way that so many mines have now disappeared, most of their locations and history lost forever. These portraits, I hope, will bring back memories to the men who once toiled in them and wonder why this once-great industry is nearly extinct, leaving in its wake thousands of men unemployed and whole communities split asunder.

Deep-mined coal is too expensive, the pundits say, and power stations and other users rely on cheaper subsidised coal from abroad and opencast coal. Existing and proposed sites will desecrate the landscape even more, leaving their scars for years to come. However, we must never forget that the 'Black Diamonds' have demanded so many sacrifices of blood, sweat and tears.

ACKNOWLEDGEMENTS

So many people have helped me in my search for the legends of the North Staffordshire coalfield, and to them I offer my gratitude. If any errors are found, then I am to blame.

A special mention I must make is for the Chatterley Whitfield Mining Museum, Tunstall, Stoke-on-Trent, and Jim Worgan, for most of the photographs and help without which this book could not have been made.

Others who have supplied material or assistance have been:

John Abberley
Alan Cookman
Colin Hutchinson
J. Jones
J.W. Shaw
F.V. Vodrey
Evening Sentinel
Steve Benz for marketing
Frank Rhodes of Lightwood for editing and proof-reading.

A.C. Baker
Vic Dodd
Jim Hutchinson
Keith Meeson
W.R. Shenton
Reg Walklate
Keele University

F. Cartlidge
Mike Hodgkinson
Will Jack
Dave Richards
Ken Stevenson
F. Sanderson
The Warrilow Collection

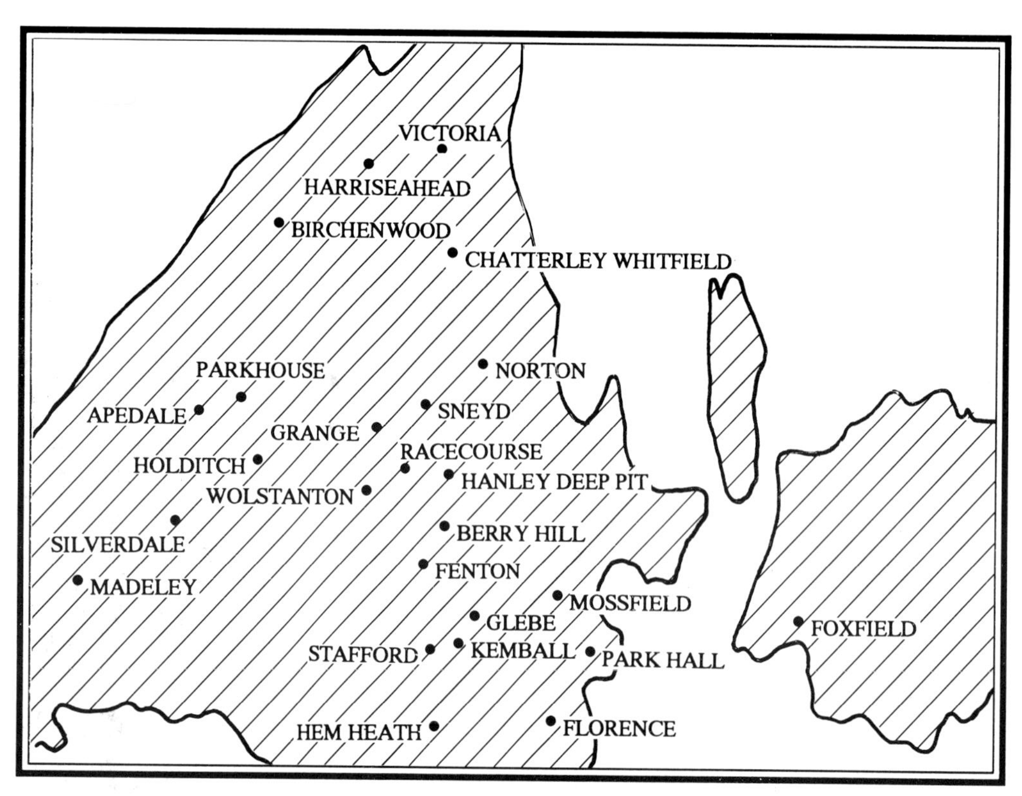

THE NORTH STAFFORDSHIRE COALFIELD

VICTORIA BIDDULPH (1850-1982), c. 1900

In May 1898 work started to widen and deepen the Magpie shaft, which was 130 yards deep and 8 feet in diameter. The work was completed in 1900 and the pit renamed Victoria.

VICTORIA BIDDULPH (1850-1982)

After the conversion in 1898, when the shaft was deepened to 477 yards and widened to 14 feet in diameter. The pit closed in 1982.

VICTORIA BIDDULPH (1850-1982), 1951

Havelock Pit, of Victoria colliery, Biddulph.

VICTORIA BIDDULPH (1850-1982), 25 October 1983

The demise of Victoria colliery. The Head gear in its death throes. Going.......

VICTORIA BIDDULPH (1850-1982), 25 October 1983

Going........ ....Gone.

The Victoria shaft took 12,000 tonnes of pit waste to fill it, and was then capped with some 867 cubic metres of concrete. The 6 feet diameter balance rope pulley wheels were donated to Biddulph Council, and were erected outside the town hall as a memorial to the once-thriving mining industry.

BIRCHENWOOD COLLIERY (c.1891-1932)

Almost all the coal from this group of pits was used for coke and other by-products. The coke was transported to Robert Heath's ironworks at Black Bull, Biddulph and Norton. There was an explosion at the No. 18 pit on 18 December 1925 which killed seven men and seriously injured 14 others. A royal visit was made to the site by their Majesties King George V and Queen Mary, who watched the discharge of coke from the ovens. Although the pits were closed c. 1932, the company still continued to produce coke and other by-products with coal from the Biddulph collieries. The last coke was made in May 1973. A few months later the plant was demolished.

THE CHATTERLEY IRON COMPANY No. 4 PIT

The photograph of this wrought iron pit frame at the Chatterley Iron Company No. 4 pit at Tunstall was taken on the occasion of the inspection made of the North Staffordshire Blackband Ironstones by the South Midland Institute of Mining, Civil and Mechanical Engineers.

CHATTERLEY WHITFIELD

There were originally two companies, Chatterley Iron Company of Talke who acquired the Whitfield Colliery in 1872. In 1884 Chatterley went into liquidation. A new company was formed and became known as Chatterley Whitfield Collieries Ltd. There were six shafts in use when the N.C.B. took over in 1947:

Engine, 150 yards deep sunk in 1863, Middle, 250 yards deep sunk in 1863,
Institute 440 yards deep sunk in 1863, Platt, 432 yards deep sunk in 1863
Winstanley, 235 yards deep sunk in 1914, Hesketh, 640 yards deep sunk in 1915

Employing some 3000 men and boys, it was the largest pit in the North Staffordshire coalfield at that time. An explosion occurred in 1881 killing 21 men and boys. The colliery was closed in 1977 and is now a mining museum.

WHITFIELD LANE 8, BRINDLEY FORD, 1920s

Early turn.

NORTON COLLIERY (1860-1877), c.1895

The coal screens and railway can be seen in the foreground with the winding engine house and the wooden head gears.

NORTON COLLIERY (1860-1977), 1912

This colliery was also referred to as Ford Green and Bellerton Lane because of its location. The photograph was taken in 1912 for a daily newspaper because there had been an explosion. Fortunately it had happened on a Saturday afternoon when only three men were at work. They were pit fettlers, men who inspect the shaft for any damage and repair it. This work was always done when the pit was not drawing coal. One of the men was killed. Overcome by the after-damp, he fell with his head overhanging the cage and was beheaded when the cage was drawn to the surface. Fifty pit ponies also perished in the explosion. If, by the grace of God, it had happened only a few hours before, when 500 men and boys were at work, it would have been the worst disaster in the coalfield. On 15 October 1915, 56 men were riding on the man-trolleys down the steep incline to the Cockshead seam when the rope broke. It took no time at all for them to travel a few hundred yards and become derailed, ending up a tangled mess of wood, steel, flesh and blood. Many died and the others were seriously injured.

NORTON COLLIERY (1860-1977), c.1950

The officials of Norton Colliery are seen here at a dinner at the George Hotel, Burslem.

SNEYD COLLIERY, 1880s

Shown here are the Landsale yard, the foreshaft sinking and the rail cutting excavation.

SNEYD COLLIERY (1887-1962)

An explosion occurred here on New Year's day 1942, killing 57 men and boys. The last coal was drawn in July 1962, and the colliery closed when the workings converged with Wolstanton Colliery. One of the shafts remained in use for ventilation purposes and as a second means of egress from the northern part of the Wolstanton mine.

GRANGE COLLIERY (c. 1860-1920)

This pit was sunk around 1860 at Rushton Grange, near Cobridge, for coal and ironstone for Robert Heath's Ironworks at Black Bull, Biddulph. Severe flooding took place in December 1917, and this also affected the Racecourse Colliery. At the time, the abandonment of the mine was considered, but, after discussions with the Shelton Co., who owned the profitable Racecourse, it was decided to install a large beam pumping engine, called the 'King Edward Pump', which drained the two pits. Shelton then acquired the Grange for this purpose. Wolstanton church can be seen on the skyline.

RACECOURSE COLLIERY (1840-1941)

This was originally the site of Hanley Racecourse, off Cobridge Road. Meetings were held in August, 'Wakes Week', and the last meeting was on 5 August 1840. Pits 3, 4 and 5 were sunk for the Earl of Granville to feed his Ironworks in Etruria, which later became known as Shelton Iron, Steel & Coal Co. Number 5 pit closed during the coal strike in 1921. Number 3 continued to draw coal and ironstone, with number 4 used as the upcast. A very wet pit due to the closure of the Grange Colliery, severe flooding took place in May 1941, and it was not re-opened. Fortunately there was no loss of life. One gets the impression that a giant eraser has obliterated this pit, like so many others. Event the two massive spoil heaps, evidence of one hundred years of toil, have vanished, used for infill and road building. The site is now part of the Festival Park.

HANLEY DEEP PIT, c.1860

These shafts were originally sunk in 1854, and were deepened and widened at the turn of the century.

HANLEY DEEP PIT (1901-1962)

After the alteration, the Deep pit lived up to its name at the time of being the deepest mine in the coalfield, and one of the deepest in the country. In its prime, during the 1930s, it employed 1552 men and boys underground and 395 working on the bank. It closed in 1962, when the underground workings were to converge with Wolstanton Colliery.

HANLEY DEEP PIT (1901-1962), 1951

The colliery is now obliterated and the site called Hanley Forest Park. As a reminder of its coal mining days, a pit winding wheel has been erected at one of the entrances, whilst the spoil heaps have been reclaimed.

HANLEY DEEP PIT (1901-1962)

This view of the pit shows the proximity to Town Road. Part of the colliery office block survives to this day.

BERRY HILL COLLIERY (1863-1960)

An explosion occurred on 12 January 1872, killing 6 men. For many years Berry Hill was the headquarters of the former Staffordshire and Western Areas of the National Coal Board. It remains the site of the Berryhill Rescue Station, and is also the subject of a public outcry against British Coal's plan to turn the site into a vast opencast mine.

FENTON, GLEBE, COLLIERY (1865-1964)

On 13 June 1963 an explosion caused by coal dust killed 3 men. Since its closure, the colliery spoil heap has been reclaimed and landscaped, and a mine care and commemorative plaque have been placed on the southern side of the site to mark its association with mining.

MOSSFIELD COLLIERY (1819-1963)

An explosion propagated by coal dust, ignited by spontaneous combustion, killed 66 men and boys on 16 October 1889. On 21 March 1940, an explosion killed 11 men, again as a result of coal dust and spontaneous combustion. The pit was known to the miners by the familiar name 'Old Sal'.

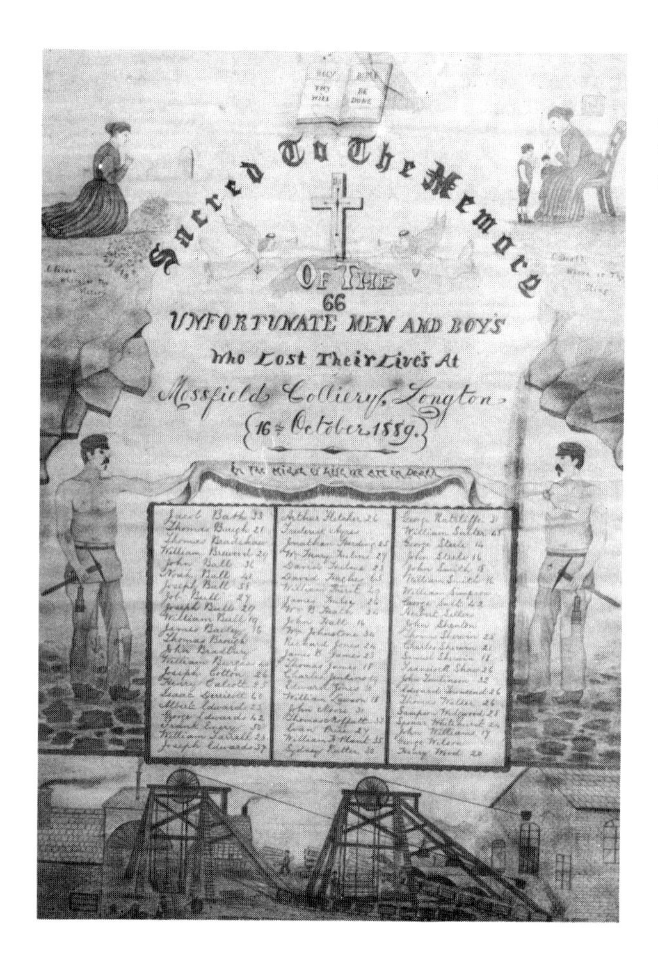

MOSSFIELD COLLIERY
(1819-1963)

This design was drawn by George Woodward in 1890, to commemorate the disaster of 16 October 1889 when 66 men and boys lost their lives.

STAFFORD COAL & IRON (1873-1969)

The company started to operate in 1873 to obtain the blackstone ironstone and coal in the upper seams. In 1874 it was decided to erect a brick works to meet the company's needs. Plans and estimates were made in 1876 for the creation of two blast furnaces to produce some 500 tons of iron per week from the Bassey Mine ironstone. The portrait shows the Sutherland Pit, the Homer Pit and the Pits and Furnaces.

STAFFORD COLLIERY (1873-1969)

There were two pits, the Homer and the Sutherland, the latter named after the Duke of Sutherland, who was chairman of the company until his death in 1892. The Homer Pit had 10 insets, was 16 feet in diameter and 607 yards deep. The Sutherland Pit had 13 insets, was 16 feet in diameter and 596 yards deep. It was only in 1877, when the colliery had progressed sufficiently, that a manager was appointed at a salary of £400 per annum. Also known as Great Fenton, it suffered an explosion on 10 April 1885, when 8 men were killed. The cause was firedamp ignited by shotfiring.

STAFFORD COLLIERY (1873-1969), 1967

The Sutherland Pit.

PARKHALL COLLIERY (1860-1962), 1940s
Situated on the outskirts of Longton, the underground workings were merged with Florence Colliery in 1962.

KEMBALL COLLIERY (1876-1963), 1940s

The picture was taken when the colliery was used as a training pit for new recruits in the mining industry. It proved very useful during World War 2 to train 'Bevin Boys'. Coal was in short supply in the latter stages of the war, so it was decided by the then Minister of Labour, Ernest Bevin, that there would be a ballot to determine whether the conscript should go into the armed services or work in the mines. They came to North Staffordshire from all walks of life. Sons of peers of the realm to the lowest labourer, no-one was given preference and all were treated the same. The shafts were known as Pender and Bourne, and for many years it served as the return airway for Hem Heath Colliery, which had only one shaft until the 1950s.

KEMBALL COLLIERY (1876-1963), c. 1960
Management and instructors' team of Kemball Training Colliery, Fenton, Stoke-on-Trent.

FLORENCE COLLIERY (1874-1990), early 1950s

Florence was named after the eldest daughter of the 3rd Duke of Sutherland, the original owner. Two shafts were sunk, and a third some time later. The photograph shows new head gears being erected over old. The colliery merged with Hem Heath Colliery in 1990 to form Trentham Colliery.

FLORENCE COLLIERY (1874-1990)

Jubilation!! The picture says it all! In two years the colliery was to be merged with Hem Heath - the Big A.

FLORENCE COLLIERY (1874-1990), 25 May 1979

An historic link-up, over half a mile underground, between Florence and Hem Heath Collieries.

FLORENCE COLLIERY (1874-1990), 31 October 1990

Another view of the modernised Florence Colliery the year it merged with Hem Heath.

HEM HEATH COLLIERY (1924-)

The Duke of Sutherland cut the first sod in July 1924 for this comparatively new pit. It was for Stafford Coal and Iron Company, of which he was the chairman, to exploit known coal reserves south of their Stafford Colliery and the Bassey Ironstone. Ventilation was a problem and it became difficult to increase output. When nationalised in 1947, it became obvious that the existing shaft arrangements were inadequate if the rich resources were to be fully exploited, so work began in 1950 to restructure the pit to make a virtually new colliery. It is interesting to note that during the modernisation, production never stopped.

HEM HEATH TRENTHAM COLLIERY (1924-1950), 'THE BIG A'

Known as 'The Big A' because of its distinctive head gear, it had been completely rebuilt on the site of the original colliery which was sunk in 1924. Work began in 1950 on sinking a new shaft, 24 feet in diameter and 1134 yards deep, the third deepest in the country. Further work was done on the original shaft in 1956 when it was extended to 20 feet in diameter and deepened to 1115 yards, shortly after the connecting roadway to Kemball Training Centre was abandoned. A drift was driven some 2900 yards for the surface for some coal output and man riding. In 1979 there were 1790 men employed, with an output of 1,001,368 tonnes. Florence Colliery merged with Hem Heath to form Trentham Colliery in 1990.

FOXFIELD COLLIERY (1880-1965)

Situated in the Cheadle coalfield, where known coal-getting goes back to the seventeenth century. Although the work started at the colliery in 1880, it was not until 1888 that the sinking was completed. The first shaft was 752 feet deep. Another shaft was sunk later at 1000 feet deep and remained the same until the colliery closed in 1965. About 1946, Foxfield employed some 390 men underground and 150 on the surface.

BIGNALL HILL COLLIERIES
JAMAGE AND ROOKERY

There are three recorded disasters at these pits: 24 December 1874 - 17 men killed. 6 July 1875 - 5 men killed, 25 November 1911 - 6 men killed. In the last, twenty-seven pit ponies also perished.

ROOKERY MINE, c. 1930

The upcast shaft.

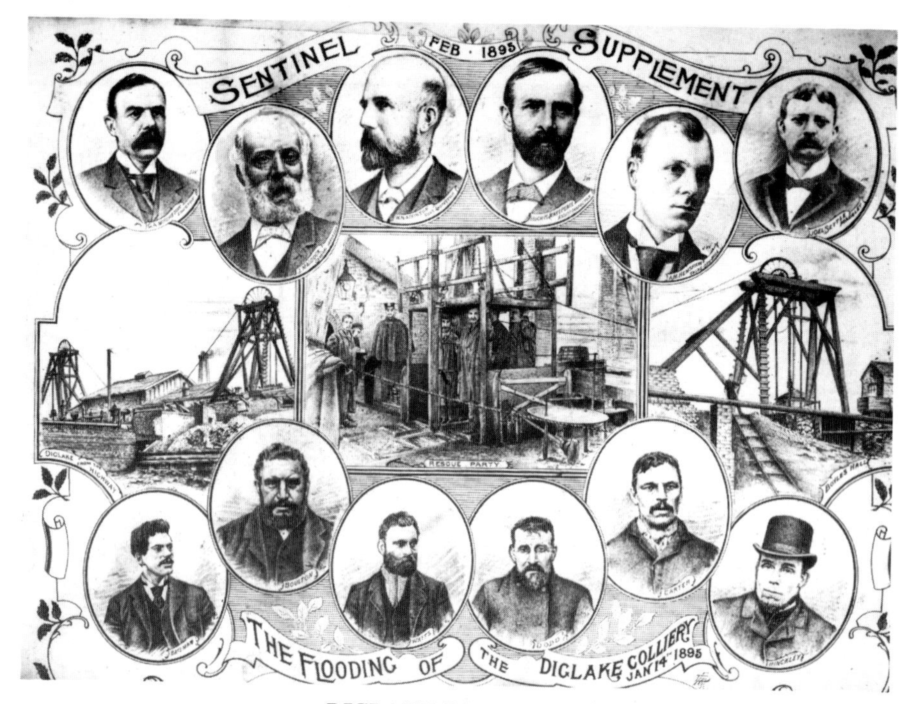

DIGLAKE COLLIERY

On 14 January 1895, one of the worst colliery disasters happened at the Diglake Colliery, Bignall Hill. Two hundred and sixty men and boys descended the pit that day. At 11.30am a spate of water from the old flooded Rookery Pit, augmented from above by the inclement weather, spewed with relentless fury into the lower regions of the Diglake mine, carrying and drowning everything in its path. Seventy-eight men and boys perished, some of the bodies never being recovered. The ones saved owed their lives to the heroic deed of the six men in the lower part of the portrait: mssrs. Bateman, Boulton, Watts, Dodd, Carter, Hinkley.

DIGLAKE COLLIERY DISASTER, 1895

On 7 March 1933 the remains of a victim were recovered after being entombed for 38 years.

DIGLAKE COLLIERY DISASTER, 1895

The funeral of one of the bodies recovered after 38 years entombment took place on 18 August 1933.

PARKHOUSE COLLIERY (1874-1968)

Situated just off the A34 near Chesterton, this colliery closed in 1968 and is now the site of the Parkhouse Industrial Estate.

BURLEY PIT, APEDALE COLLIERY (c.1850-1926), c. 1900

Burley Pit, 23 March 1878, 23 miners killed; 20 June 1878, 9 miners killed; Sladderhill, 2 April 1891, 10 miners killed. All were caused by explosions resulting from firedamp being ignited by shotfiring.

WOLSTANTON COLLIERY (1920-1985), c. 1950

This photograph shows the colliery before modernisation, when it was to be deemed the 'Superpit' of the North Staffordshire coalfield, drawing coal from three redundant collieries: Chatterley Whitfield, Hanley Deep Pit and Sneyd. A group of pottery manufacturers financed the sinking of the shafts which were the deepest coalmining shafts in western Europe.

WOLSTANTON COLLIERY (1920-1985), 1957

Work in progress to modernise.

WOLSTANTON COLLIERY (1920-1985), 1958
Work in progress to modernise.

WOLSTANTON COLLIERY (1920-1985), 1961

The Shaft Sinkers - showing the men who sank the new shaft at Wolstanton. The shaft was commissioned in 1961 and on completion was equipped with two tower-mounted Koepe winding engines, each with a cage and balance weight. It was 24 feet in diameter and 1139 yards deep. The existing upcast shaft was enlarged and deepened to 1145 yards deep, the deepest coal mine shaft at that time in Britain, equipped again with a tower-mounted Koepe winder.

COAL CUTTING OF YESTERYEAR

This picture shows a scraper chain.

COAL CUTTING OF YESTERYEAR

An Anderson Boyes electric coal cutter of the 1930s. It was capable of undercutting a 150-yard length in a 7-hour shift with a team of two men.

COAL CUTTING OF YESTERYEAR

A Jeffrey electric coal cutter of the 1920s.

COAL CUTTING OF YESTERYEAR

An Anderson Boyes 15 middle cutter of the 1930s

COAL CUTTING OF YESTERYEAR

HOLDITCH COLLIERY (1912-1989)

The colliery was known locally as 'Brymbo'. There were two shafts, No. 1 sunk in 1916, and No. 2 sunk in 1912. They were both approximately 2000 feet deep. The two main seams were Great Row and the Four Feet. An explosion occurred in the Four Feet seam on Friday 2 July 1937, when 30 men were killed and 8 injured. Extensive modernisation took place after 1947 using some of the most modern machinery. The colliery was reputed to be the most gassy in Britain. From July 1976 it supplied 1.25million therms of gas per year, equivalent to 4000 tons of coal, to local brickworks, firing some ½ million bricks per week.

HOLDITCH COLLIERY (1912-1989), February 1958

Miners wait with officials to make the descent at Holditch Colliery.

HOLDITCH COLLIERY (1912-1989), 1950s

Fireman Jack Meeson seen with two haulage hands at the bottom of the Four Foot Dip. A few yards further on the left of the picture is the sealed entrance where the explosion had occurred in 1937.

SILVERDALE COLLIERY (c.1830-), c. 1918

The Silverdale Company was formed in 1792 to exploit the Silverdale and Leycett area, mostly for ironstone to supply Ralph Sneyd's Ironworks at Knutton Heath. Coal was drawn at Silverdale as early as 1830, to provide coal for the Silverdale Ironworks. There have been three recorded disasters: 7 July 1870, 19 men killed; 22 December 1872, 8 men killed; 6 April 1876, 5 men killed. The colliery started a mechanisation programme in 1950 with the application of the Meco Moor Cutter-loader, and in the Peacock seam production was obtained with A.B. Trepan shearers.

SILVERDALE COLLIERY (c.1830-)

Tandem headgear single cage system, No. 14 upcast shafts.

KENTS LANE PIT, SILVERDALE

KENTS LANE, SILVERDALE, 1896

SILVERDALE COLLIERY (c.1830-)

ACHIEVEMENT. Three of the pit men who made it possible discuss their achievement in backing Britain's productivity drive, and putting the pit back on its feet after a bad spell. Frank Deakin, Bill Edgeley and John Amesbury.

MADELEY COLLIERY (1880-1957)

This colliery was also known as Leycett. There were two explosions at the Fair Lady pit: 21 January 1880, 62 killed; 16 October 1883, 6 killed. Both were caused by ignition by shot-firing.

MINNIE PIT, c. 1872

The Minnie Pit of the Podmore Colliery, Halmerend is shown during the celebration of the opening day. The first sod was cut in 1871, and the pit was named after Minnie Craig, daughter of one of the owners. This pit will ever be remembered as the most infamous in the North Staffordshire coal field due to the heavy loss of life it incurred. Three explosions have been recorded in its history: 6 February 1898, this happened on a Sunday when fortunately no one was at work, but all the pit ponies perished; 17 January 1915, 9 miners killed; 12 January 1918, 155 miners killed.

MINNIE PIT EXPLOSION,
17 January 1915

This was the second explosion on a Sunday when fortunately only 27 men were at work. Nine men were killed and many were severely injured.

MINNIE PIT EXPLOSION,
12 January 1918

The Apedale Colliery No.1 rescue team are seen about to descend the Minnie Pit after the explosion on 12 January 1918.

MINNIE PIT EXPLOSION, 12 January 1918

The Midland Coal, Coke and Iron Company's Rescue Team photographed just before descending the Minnie Pit at Halmerend to recover the bodies of those killed in the explosion on 12 January 1918.

MINNIE PIT, 19 January 1918

The pit is seen here a few days after the explosion.

LAMP CHECKS

The lamp checks illustrated were used mostly for identification purposes in case of accident. They were exchanged for the miner's lamp bearing the same number. The collection shows checks from some of the collieries featured in this book. Also shown are some badges of the North Staffs. Miners' Federation, and a pay check.

LAMP SAFETY TEST

Having received his lamp from the lamphouse, young Jack Holdcroft hands it to an official to test for safety. (Jack started work at Chatterley Whitfield in 1933, and in retirement acted as a guide at the mining museum until 1991.)

CONTRABAND CHECK

Young David is subjected to a search for contraband, i.e. cigarettes and matches. If any were found he would have been instantly dismissed.

THE MORE WE ARE TOGETHER, c. 1920s

A happy band of miners pose for the photographer just before descending. The picture was probably taken just after a lay-off.

WINDING ENGINE AT BROWN LEES COLLIERY, c. 1900

The winding engine at Brown Lees Colliery at the turn of the century, on which can be seen the chalk markings on the drum and the rope. These were indications to the engine man that when the white mark on the rope tallied with B/D, the bottom deck of the cage was at the pit bottom, the T/D marking indicating the top deck. The engine men took great pride in the winding engine and the engine house. Both were scrupulously clean, the brass on the engine highly polished, the ironwork cleaned with an oily rag. The cleaning material and brush can be seen on the far wall.

INTO THE ABYSS

At the pit head the banks man is about to signal the winding engine man to lower the cage. The cage will plummet with its human cargo at an average rate of 70 feet per second.

PIT BOTTOM

At the pit bottom the onsetter is signalling for the empty cage to be drawn up to bring down another load of pitmen.

HAULAGE c. 1911

The beast of burden with its minder is seen in this photograph taken before the systems of the endless rope and conveyor. The pony drivers, all boys, had a great respect for them. The ponies only saw daylight one week in twelve months, when miners had their annual week's holiday. Hundreds of ponies were maimed and killed.

SNAPPIN' TIME

Welcome refreshment for both hard workers.

THE 'JIG'

This is pictured at the top of a 'Jig' dip. To save mechanical power a 'Jig' uses the weight of the full tubs descending to pull empty tubs up the dip. A 'Jig' is like a large pulley, as shown, with the steel rope wound round it three or four times and an iron band acting as a brake to control the speed. The dip or gradient can be as much as 1 in 6, which illustrates the success of the 'Jig', a very economical device. The overman in the picture is apparently tired after walking up the dip.

COAL GETTING, March 1960

Here is a typical haulage scene near to the coal face. Tubs are being filled by conveyor before being hauled outbye to the pit bottom by means of the endless rope. The chain on the ground was used for 'lashing' the loaded tubs on. The journey, as it was called, consisting of between 10 and 15 loaded tubs, could travel 2 to 3 miles before reaching its destination. Empty tubs would be travelling inbye to replace those used. This continuous cycle went on all day: loaded tubs going out, empties coming in. The haulage system was operated by young miners. At the time of this picture, they would be between 14 and 18 years of age.

COAL GETTING, March 1960

Coal is seen here coming from the coal face on to a conveyor belt, as water is sprayed to keep down the dust in order to eliminate the danger of spontaneous combustion.

COAL GETTING, c. 1960

This conveyor belt with motor is carrying coal from the coal face in the Bullhurst seam at Norton Colliery. This was the first face worked on the retreat system.

COAL GETTING

In the days before the arrival of the coal-cutting machine a collier can be seen undercutting the coal with a pick. The lamp hanging on a prop was his only source of illumination, about a half candlepower, and his indicator of the presence of dangerous gas.

COAL GETTING, c. 1873

Colliers 'hand holing' while the manager looks on.

WHEN DAY IS DONE

Before the days of pit-head baths, a miner, still in his dirt, is seen having a meal with his family.

WHEN DAY IS DONE

Getting the dirt off in the tin bath in front of the fire.

WHEN DAY IS DONE,
September 1942

This is a miner's pay slip for seven days hard graft. Probably he was considered fortunate, for most men of his age were in the armed services, but his part was as vital to the war effort as were the armed forces, and so many miners gave their lives too.

Madeley Collieries Limited 19 SEP 1942

No 366.

Wages of F. Cartledge

	£	s	d.	£	s.	d.
6 5/8 Days @ 5/9	1	18	2			
Add 44 %		16	9			
,, 1/- per day		6				
,, 2/8 War Wage		16				
,, 1/- Attend. Bon.		6				
Green Award ...		16	7			
..............Bonus						
Deductions				4	19	6
Baths			2			
Health Ins.		1	0			
Employ Ins			10			
Hospitals ...			3			
Union Contrib....			6			
Coal			1			
Rent						
Income Tax						
				4	16	10

TRANSPORT OF THE 'BLACK DIAMONDS'

The Institute and Platt headgears at Chatterley Whitfield form a backdrop to a scene of railway wagons being filled with coal after it has been screened.

TRANSPORT OF THE 'BLACK DIAMONDS'

Roger was one of the many locomotives that pulled, shoved and shunted the wagons from wharves and main line sidings to and from the pit head. They were used also as collier trains to bring miners from the Potteries to Whitfield and Biddulph.

TRANSPORT OF THE 'BLACK DIAMONDS', c. 1930s

Locomotive *Edward* seen pulling loaded coal wagons from Chatterley Whitfield.

TRANSPORT OF THE 'BLACK DIAMONDS', c. 1960

A coal train from Chatterley Whitfield is heading for Ford Green crossings.

TRANSPORT OF THE 'BLACK DIAMONDS', c. 1970s

This shows the last coal train from Chatterley Whitfield.

RESCUE TEAMS - THE VALIANTS

Chatterley Whitfield No. 4 Rescue Brigade.

RESCUE TEAMS - THE VALIANTS, c. 1920s

'Greater love of men hath no man than this, that a man lay down his life for his friends.' St John, chapter 15, verse 13. Midland Rescue Brigade No. 3 are shown with the caged canaries who gave early warning of the danger of gas.

THE CARNEGIE HERO FUND MEDAL

This medal was presented to Harry Bickerton and Thomas Gleaves who, at considerable risk to their own lives, rescued six men who were overcome by carbon monoxide gas at New Hem Heath Colliery, Chesterton, on 25 February 1915. They tried in vain to rescue the remaining 12 men, who were unfortunately suffocated, before being overcome themselves and being brought to the surface by the rescue team.

THE CARNEGIE HERO FUND MEDAL

The obverse of the medal awarded to Harry Bickerton and Thomas Gleaves.

THE STRIKE OF '26

For the first time in our history the industrial life of Britain came to a standstill on 4 May 1926. Probably between 3 and 4 million workers obeyed their Trade Unions and ceased work when a General Strike was declared in sympathy with the miners. The mine owners told the M.F.G.B. that they were facing great losses, and that miners were to take a loss in their wages and work longer hours. The union, headed by Herbert Smith, told them 'Nowt doin'' and that the men were already 'stripped to the bone'. The T.U.C. terminated their part in the strike on 12 May and the miners were left to battle alone. Seven long months of deprivation and despair followed. Near to starvation, some of the miners, knowing the geology of the area, dug shafts to reach seams of outcrop coal. These areas became 'little Klondykes'. The coal was sold and the money used to buy food for their families. Pictured above is a group of miners taking five minutes at their outcrop.

THE STRIKE OF '26

Another outcrop scene shows 'Jim Slack's hole' at Cheadle. Many casualties occurred in the outcrops, men being buried alive because the could not afford the timber for supports. How history repeats itself!! The big consumers were buying cheaper subsidised coal from abroad, while pit closures here were throwing human flotsam on the scrapheap.

THE STRIKE OF '26

More striking miners at their outcrop in the 'Ollies, now Hanley Forest Park.

THE STRIKE OF '26

This group of striking miners did well during the strike. Their weekly wage before the strike was about 30 shillings (£1.50). The younger ones earned about 15 shillings (£0.75). Now they were the coal owners, making some £20.00 a week. They were able to refurbish their cottages, bought new furniture and even a new piano.

RETIREMENT

Ready for a well-earned rest, these ex-miners are receiving their long service certificates on retirement. Some had worked in the pit for 50 years.

PARKHALL MALE VOICE CHOIR, 1992

The choir was formed in 1950 as the Parkhall Colliery Male Voice Choir, and although the colliery closed in 1962, the choir has continued in its present form, giving concerts in halls and churches throughout the area. *Back row l to r*: John Humphries, Derek Daly, Dave Mellor, Horace Hodson, George Mulvey, George Johnson, Alex Brown, Joe Shaw, Ken Fricke, Ted Williams, George Pass
Middle row l to r: Harry Johnson, Dave Powner, Tony Middleton, Vic Arnold, Joe Sidley, Dennis Dutton. Jim Breward, Stan Goodwin, Bill Leighton, Tony Capper, Ron Fricke, Bill Walker
Front row l to r: Jack Smallwood, Tom Street, John Neale, Cyril Cope, Harry Cartlidge, Bob Slinn (Conductor), Rex Morse, Alf Shaw, Ernie Wakefield, Eric Wain, Duncan MacPherson.

KNOWN MINES FROM 1875

CHEADLE AREA

Callow Hill
Cheadle Park
Common Side
Consall
Cross Flats
Delphouse
Dilhorne
Foxfield
Hazlewall
Ipstones
Lady's Well
Litley
Little Above Park
Mosey Moor
New Haden
Park Hall
Racecourse
Well Street
Woodhead

LONGTON/TRENTHAM AREA

Adderley Green
Anchor
Bentilee
Brownsfield
Fenton - Glebe
Fenton Park
Florence
Foley
Gainmore
Goldenhill
Hem Heath
Hill Top
Homer Hill
Hulme Valley
Kemball
Longton Hall
Meir Hay
Meir Heath
Mossfield
Old Field
Parkhall
Stafford - Dukes
Stone Road
Ubberley Hall
Weston Coyney
Willfield

HANLEY AREA

Bellsmill
Berry Hill
Blakelow
Boothen
Botteslow
Brookhouse
Bucknall
Bucknall Church
Far Green
Foxhole
Foxley
Greasley
Greasleyside
Hall
Hanley & Bucknall
Hanley Deep Pit
Ivy House
Joiner's Square
Lady's Well
Lawn
Northwood
Pear Tree
Racecourse
Rowhurst
Slippery Lane
Tinkersclough
Townsend
Wetley Moor

NEWCASTLE AND KIDSGROVE AREA

Apedale	Glass House	Knutton Farm	New Hem Heath	Slappenfield
Bathpool	Harecastle	Lawton	Oldcote	Speedwell
Bignall Hill	Head o' th' Lane	Leycett	Old Hays Wood	Talk o' the Hill
Birchenwood	Highcarr	Madeley	Old Oak	The Grove
Brown	Holditch	Maryhill	Park House	The Nabs
Bunkers Hill	Hollin Wood	Miles Green	Podmore Hall	Valentine
Burley	Holly Wood	Millbank	Racecourse	Watermills
Chesterton	Jamage	Minnie	Ravenscliff	Whitebarn
Clough Hall	Kidsgrove	Moss	Rookery	Wolstanton
Crackley	Kidswood	Nelson	Rosemary Hill	Woodshutts
Diglake	Knutton	Newfield	Silverdale	

BIDDULPH AREA

Baileys	Brown Lees	Meadows Stile	Red Cross	Tower Hill
Biddulph Valley	Childerplay	New Pool	Stonetrough	Victoria
Black Bull	Hall o' Lee	Park Farm	Top Falls	Woodhouse
Bradeley Green	Lancasters			

BURSLEM AREA

Bank Top	Grange	Jackfield	Sandbach	Sneyd Green
Bradeley	Hamil	Mill Hayes	Sneyd	Stanfield
Bycars	Hill Top	New Hayes	Sneyd Farm	Watkins
Cobridge				

TUNSTALL AREA

Ashwood	Goldendale	Lowlands	Packmoor	Tileries
Brownhills	Goldenhill	Mays	Pinnox	Trubshaw
Chalky	Greenfields	New Chapel	Ridgeway	Turnhurst
Chatterley	Greenhead	Newfield	Rising Lark	Wedgwood
Chell	Harriseahead	Outclough	Scotia	Whitfield
Clanway	High Lane	Oxford	Thursfield	Yeldhill
Furlong	Lane Ends			

NORTON AREA

LEEK AREA

Corn Hill	Ford Green	Norton	Rectory	Shaffalong

PIT DISASTERS FROM 1855

The following is a record of colliery disasters in North Staffordshire since 1855, in which at least five were killed:

DATE	COLLIERY	LOCATION	NUMBER KILLED
25 May 1855	Oldfield	Longton	7
29 Jan 1859	Bycars	Burslem	5
2 Mar 1864	Brookhouse	Hanley	5
1 Mar 1865	Clough Hall	Kidsgrove	5
13 Dec 1866	Talk o' th' Hill	Newcastle	91
11 Nov 1867	Homer Hill	Longton	12
7 Jul 1870	Silverdale	Newcastle	19
12 Jan 1871	Leycett	Newcastle	8
12 Mar 1872	Berry Hill	Stoke	6
Dec 1872	Silverdale	Newcastle	8
18 Feb 1873	Talk o'th' Hill	Newcastle	18
24 Dec 1874	Bignall Hill	Audley	17
30 Apr 1875	Bunkers Hill	Kidsgrove	43
6 Jul 1875	Jamage	Chesterton	5
6 Apr 1876	Silverdale	Newcastle	5
23 Mar 1878	Apedale	Newcastle	23

DATE	COLLIERY	LOCATION	NUMBER KILLED
12 Sep 1879	Leycett	Newcastle	8
21 Jan 1880	Leycett	Newcastle	62
7 Feb 1881	Whitfield	Tunstall	21
16 Oct 1883	Leycett	Newcastle	6
10 Apr 1885	Great Fenton	Stoke	8
20 Jun 1885	Apedale	Newcastle	9
18 Oct 1889	Mossfield	Longton	64
2 Apr 1891	Apedale	Newcastle	10
14 Jan 1895	Diglake	Audley	78
25 Nov 1911	Jamage	Chesterton	6
15 Jan 1915	Minnie	Halmerend	9
25 Feb 1915	New Hem Heath	Chesterton	12
12 Jan 1918	Minnie	Halmerend	155
18 Dec 1925	Birchenwood	Kidsgrove	7
2 Jul 1937	Holditch	Newcastle	30
21 Mar 1940	Mossfield	Longton	11
1 Jan 1942	Sneyd	Burslem	57

Other local titles published by S.B. Publications in the series 'A Portrait in Old Picture Postcard's:

Bootle, Vols 1 & 2
Liverpool, Vols 1 & 2
Old Bebington
Rock Ferry, New Ferry and Bebington
Southport

Chester, Vols 1 & 2
Crewe
The Villages of West Cheshire
The Dane Valley

Bury
The Bridgewater Canal
The Lost Villages of Manchester
The Manchester Ship Canal

Aston Villa
Bournville
Pershore and District
Stourbridge and District
The Black Country, Vols 1 & 2
Walsall and District
Wolverhampton, Vols 1 & 2

Aberystwyth, Vols 1 & 2
Bangor
Chirk
Chirk and the Glyn Valley Tramway
Connah's Quay & Shotton
Denbigh
Hawarden
Llandudno
Llangollen
Rhyl
Ruthin and District
Snowdonia
Wrexham and District

Bridgnorth
Oswestry and District
Shrewsbury
Wellington

Jarrow and Hebburn

Other local titles available and in preparation. For full details send SAE to:
S.B. Publications, Unit 2, The Old Station Yard, Pipe Gate, Market Drayton, Shropshire, TF9 4HY.